Henry Grey

A Bird's Eye View of English Literature

From the Seventh Century to the Present Time

Henry Grey

A Bird's Eye View of English Literature
From the Seventh Century to the Present Time

ISBN/EAN: 9783337208851

Printed in Europe, USA, Canada, Australia, Japan

Cover: Foto ©Thomas Meinert / pixelio.de

More available books at **www.hansebooks.com**

A BIRD'S-EYE VIEW OF
ENGLISH LITERATURE.

OPINIONS OF THE PRESS.

'We heartily recommend the book.'—*American Traveller*.

'Well arranged and most useful for students.'—*Arbroath Guide*.

'Will arouse the curiosity of chance readers.'—*Banffshire Journal*.

'An eminently useful work.'—*Bath Argus*.

'Will be sure to take a prominent position.'—*Berwick Warder*.

'Will acquaint the reader in an hour with the leading facts of English Literature.'—*Boston Guardian*.

'A useful help to a general idea of English Literature.'—*Brighton Guardian*.

'Many a student will gladly invest in this little book.'—*Cape Argus*.

'Very well done.'—*Christian Age*.

'Mr. Grey has taken pains with his work, which will be generally useful.'—*Church Times*.

'Displays a wonderful amount of painstaking research.'—*Clifton Chronicle*.

'Will be a boon to students and others with bad memories.'—*Daily Chronicle*.

'Will be of great value in our schools and homes.'—*Derbyshire Advertiser*.

'A very clear synopsis.'—*Druids' Journal*.

'Well calculated to answer its purpose.'—*Ecclesiastical Gazette*.

'A capital shilling's worth.'—*Evangelical Magazine*.

'Recommended for its conciseness.'—*Glasgow Herald*.

'As useful to scholars as students.'—*Guernsey News*.

'A concise picture of English Literature.'—*Harper's Magazine*.

'Mr. Grey has the knack of including a great deal within a small compass.'—*Hereford Times.*

'A perfect *multum in parvo.*'—*Jersey Express.*

'A dainty little volume.'—*Life.*

'It is marvellous how much Mr. Grey has compressed within narrow limits.'—*Literary World.*

'Without a rival as a valuable compendium.'—*Louth Times.*

'Will impress itself on the minds of readers.'—*Marlborough Times.*

'A most handy and admirably compiled little work.'—*Malvern News.*

'Contains a surprising amount of valuable information.'—*Melbourne Portfolio.*

'A brief but interesting survey.'—*Methodist.*

'Will recall many intellectual feasts to those of mature years, and inspire the young with a desire to read the books named.'—*Mona's Herald.*

'Useful to readers of all ages.'—*Montrose Standard.*

'A valuable aid to students.'—*Northern Ensign.*

'A well-digested compilation.'—*Oban Times.*

'Of inestimable value to students.'—*Oxford Chronicle.*

'Accurate and well-executed.'—*Paisley Herald.*

'Supplies an often felt want.'—*Penrith Advertiser.*

'An exceedingly useful work.'—*People's Journal, Dundee.*

'Well fitted to impart a general knowledge of English Literature.'—*Perthshire Advertiser.*

'A good idea admirably carried out.'—*Portsmouth Times.*

'As perfect as possible.'—*Public Opinion.*

'An excellent little book for reference.'—*Quebec Chronicle.*

'Concise and handy for examination purposes.'—*Reading Mercury*.

'Very clear and accurate.'—*Schoolmaster*.

'Arranged to convey information at a glance.'—*Scottish Guardian*.

'A capital synopsis admirably condensed.'—*Sheffield Independent*.

'We cannot too strongly recommend the book.'—*Shrewsbury Journal*.

'A brief but valuable little work.'—*Society*.

'Represents a vast amount of careful research.'—*Somerset County Gazette*.

'A bright-eyed bird ; exactly meets the want of thousands.'—*Sword & Trowel*.

'Brings the entire range of English Literature within the focus of the reader's eye.'—*Surrey Gazette*.

'A novel idea thoroughly well worked out.'—*Tiverton Times*.

'An intelligently-compiled synopsis.'—*Toronto Mail*.

'Invaluable to students and readers generally.'—*Wiltshire Times*.

'An excellent *résumé*, accurate and pithy.'—*Winchester Observer*.

'Condensed in a very clear and lucid manner.'—*Windsor and Eton Gazette*.

'Of incalculable value to those whose reading time is limited.'—*Woolwich Journal*.

'Another most useful work by Mr. Grey.'—*Y. Greal*.

'Will be welcome to all classes.'—*York Chronicle*.

'Very accurate and reliable.'—*Yorkshire Post*.

NEW EDITION.

A BIRD'S-EYE VIEW OF
ENGLISH LITERATURE,

FROM THE SEVENTH CENTURY TO THE PRESENT TIME.

BY

HENRY GREY,

F.R.B.S., F.Z.S., F.I.Inst.,

AUTHOR OF

'AN EPITOME OF THE BIBLE,'
'THE CLASSICS FOR THE MILLION,' 'A KEY TO THE WAVERLEY NOVELS,'
'TROWEL, CHISEL, AND BRUSH,' 'A POCKET ENCYCLOPÆDIA,'
'THE PLOTS OF OLD ENGLISH PLAYS,'
'RESTING WITHOUT RUSTING,' 'ZOO NOTES,'
'SCIENCE NOTES,'
'FOR CONVERSATION WITH THE DEAF,'
'SIXTY-FIVE YEARS' REMINISCENCES,'
ETC., ETC.

SIXTH THOUSAND.

LONDON :
SWAN SONNENSCHEIN & CO., LIM.
1899.

' As 'tis a greater mystery in the art
  Of painting to foreshorten any part
  Than draw it out, so 'tis in books the chief
  Of all perfections to be plain and brief.'

S. BUTLER.

PREFACE.

IN this age of learning, when an acquaintance with English Literature is insisted on at every educational test and competitive examination, and will, in the coming generation, be as indispensable as a knowledge of spelling and grammar, it is thought that the following Synopsis of the names of our most celebrated poets and prose writers, with the dates of their birth and death, their social position, and the titles of their principal works, may prove useful not only to students, but to all who are anxious to acquire a general idea of the gradual expansion of thought and development of literary talent in the British dominions, since the days when the preaching of St. Augustine moderated the warlike propensities, and awakened the intellectual powers of our Anglo-Saxon ancestors.

H. G.

A BIRD'S-EYE VIEW

OF

ENGLISH LITERATURE.

—◆—

Authors' Names, and Dates of Birth and Death.	*Social position, and short description of their principal works.*
CAEDMON, (A.D. 610-680),	the earliest known Anglo-Saxon whose works are preserved, was a monk at Whitby, and wrote *A Paraphrase,* in verse, from the Bible, selecting the most vivid and picturesque incidents as his themes.

BEDE,
NAMED THE
VENERABLE,
(673-735),

the father of English learning,
spent his life in a monastery
at Jarrow, where he obtained
great repute as a scholar and
teacher. He wrote, in Latin,
*A Treatise on the Nature of
Things*, and *A Church History
of the English Nation*.

ALCUIN,
(735-804),

was a schoolmaster at York,
and, after a journey to Rome,
resided for some years at the
court of Charlemagne. He
was the author of several
works, in Latin, on theology,
history, mathematics, poetry,
and rhetoric.

JOANNES SCOTUS,
ERIGENA,
(810-875),

was a native of Ireland, and
the greatest philosopher of the
dark ages. He wrote a treatise on *Natural Science*, several
theological commentaries, and
some poetry.

KING ALFRED,
THE GREAT,
(849-901),

was taught by his mother, and
translated the works of several
Latin writers for the instruc-

KING ALFRED, THE GREAT, (849-901) *continued.*

tion of his subjects. He is also supposed to have originated the first *Anglo-Saxon Chronicles.*

AELFRIC, (930-1005),

a monk, and afterwards Archbishop of Canterbury, wrote *Homilies* on the doctrines of the Anglo-Saxon Church, and made translations from the Old Testament.

WILLIAM OF MALMESBURY, (1095-1143),

an Oxford priest, wrote *A History of the Early Kings and Prelates of England*, in Latin, and other works.

GEOFFREY OF MONMOUTH, (1102-1154),

Bishop of St. Asaph, compiled *A History of Britain*, based upon older records and Welsh Legends, which became very popular.

LAYAMON, (1130-1190),

a Worcestershire priest, was the author of a metrical *History of the Colonisation of*

LAYAMON, (1130-1190) *continued.*	*Britain,* named *The Brut,* which is valuable as a specimen of the transition from Anglo-Saxon to Early English.
RANULF, DE GLANVILLE, (1135-1190),	Chief Justice to Henry II., compiled the earliest *Treatise on the Laws and Customs of England.*
WALTER MAPES, (1143-1210),	Archdeacon of Oxford, wrote *The Poems of Golias,* a satire on the clergy, *Court Anecdotes,* containing sketches of the manners of his time, and contributions to *The Romances of King Arthur,* whose exploits were sung by the Welsh bards, and became the theme for many mediæval and modern poems.
ALEXANDER OF HALES, (1185-1245),	a friar, was the author of an exhaustive *Theological Treatise,* which was adopted in all the schools of Christendom.

MATTHEW PARIS, (1195-1259),	a monk of St. Alban's, wrote *A History of the World* from the Creation, which included a record of events in his own lifetime, and is considered a very valuable work.
ROGER BACON, (1214-1292),	a Franciscan monk, devoted himself to chemical, physical, and mathematical science. His great work is his *Opus Majus*, the encyclopædia of the thirteenth century. He was also acquainted with astronomy and geography, and several ancient languages.
ROBERT OF GLOUCESTER, (1230-1299),	a monk, composed a rhyming *Chronicle of English History*, consisting of more than ten thousand lines, in the vernacular language of his time.
JOHN DUNS SCOTUS, (1265-1308),	a professor at Oxford, was an eminent scholar, and earned

JOHN DUNS SCOTUS, the name of the 'Subtle
(1265-1308)   Doctor.' He wrote numerous
continued.   *Commentaries* on theological
and philosophical questions.

NICHOLAS TRIVET,   a Dominican monk, was the
(1285-1328),   author of a well-written and
trustworthy series of *Historical
Annals*, embracing a period of
nearly two centuries.

ROBERT MANNING,   a Lincolnshire monk, was the
(1272-1338),   author of a rhyming *Historical
Chronicle* in quaint early En-
glish, evincing considerable
poetical power.

WILLIAM OF OCCAM,   a Franciscan monk, earned
(1280-1347),   great reputation as a scholar
and philosopher.   He wrote
several *Theological Treatises*,
and supported the German
Emperor in his controversies
with the Pope.

RANULF HIGDEN, (1280-1367), a Benedictine monk, wrote *A Chronicle*, in Latin called *Polychronicon*, a translation of which, by Trevisa, was afterwards completed and printed by Caxton.

SIR JOHN MANDEVILLE, (1300-1372), a physician, was the author of one of the earliest known works in English prose, consisting of a narrative of his *Travels in the East*, during a period of thirty-four years.

JOHN OF FORDUN, (1310-1384), a priest at Aberdeen, wrote *A Chronicle of Scotland* from the time of Noah.

REV. JOHN WYCLIFFE, (1320-1384), an energetic promoter of the Reformation, wrote treatises against the errors of the Papacy, and made the first complete *English Translation of the Bible*.

JOHN BARBOUR,
(1319-1395),
Archdeacon of Aberdeen, was the first Scotch poet who used the English language. He wrote *The Bruce*, a chronicle of the career of the famous King of that name.

WILLIAM LANGLAND,
(1332-1399),
an Oxford fellow, was the author of an allegorical poem, entitled *The Vision of Piers Plowman*, in which he satirises the corruptions of the Church, and depicts various types of human character. The metre is alliterative, several words in each line commencing with the same letter.

GEOFFREY CHAUCER,
(1340-1400),
a courtier and diplomatist, established his fame as the first great English poet by his *Canterbury Tales*, a vivid picture of society in the fourteenth century, and several other works.

JOHN GOWER, (1320-1408),

a lawyer, exposed the vices of all classes in two poems, entitled *The Voice of one Crying*, and *The Confessions of a Lover*.

JOHN LYDGATE, (1370-1430),

a Benedictine monk, was a scholar and poet. His three chief works are *Troy Book*, *The Story of Thebes*, imitated from Chaucer, *Falls of Princes* and *London Lackpenny*, a satire.

KING JAMES I. OF SCOTLAND, (1391-1436),

while a prisoner in England composed a poem, entitled *The King's Quhair*, in praise of the lady whom he afterwards married.

REGINALD PECOCK, (1395-1460),

Bishop of Chichester, was one of the first advocates for liberty of thought on unessential religious doctrines.

SIR THOMAS LITTLETON, (1409-1481),

an eminent judge, was the author of a celebrated work on *Tenures*.

B

SIR JOHN FORTESCUE, (1395-1485),

Chief Justice to Henry VI., wrote a learned treatise on *The Common Law of England.*

ROBERT HENRYSON, (1423-1495),

a Scottish poet, was the author of *The Testament of Cresseid*, a metrical translation of *Æsop's Fables*, and some ballads.

JOHN COLET, (1466-1519),

Dean of St. Paul's, was a zealous promoter of the revival of learning, and wrote several theological and classical treatises.

WILLIAM DUNBAR, (1460-1520),

of St. Andrew's University, commemorated the marriage of James IV. in a poem entitled *The Thistle and Rose.* He also wrote a satire named *The Dance of the Seven Deadly Sins*, and other works.

GAWIN DOUGLAS, (1474-1522),

Bishop of Dunkeld, produced the first English translation of *Virgil's Æneid.*

Sir Thomas More, (1478-1535),

Chancellor to Henry VIII., wrote *Utopia*, an imaginary form of government, in Latin, and some controversial tracts in elegant English.

William Tyndale, (1477-1536),

a preacher to the English Factory at Antwerp, made *A Translation of the New Testament*, and was the author of several theological treatises in favour of the Reformation.

Sir Thomas Wyat, (1503-1542),

a courtier, composed *Sonnets*, imitated from Italian poetry, in more polished language than any previous writers.

Henry Howard, Earl of Surrey, (1517-1547),

wrote elegant *Love Sonnets*, and translated part of *The Æneid* in blank verse.

Alexander Barclay, (1476-1552),

a Benedictine monk, was the translator of *The Ship of Fools*, a celebrated German satire, and of *Sallust's Jugurthine War*.

JOHN LELAND, (1506-1552),

Chaplain to Henry VIII., and the first English Antiquary, wrote *An Itinerary* of his travels, and other works.

SIR DAVID LYNDSAY, (1490-1555),

a Jacobite courtier, was the author of *The Dream*, and other satirical poems.

HUGH LATIMER, (1490-1555),

Bishop of Worcester, was celebrated for his quaint *Sermons in favour of the Reformation.*

THOMAS CRANMER, (1489-1556),

Archbishop of Canterbury, wrote several *Controversial Treatises*, and *A Catechism.*

JOHN BALE, (1495-1563),

Bishop of Ossory, wrote *Miracle Plays*, and compiled *A Summary of British Authors* in Latin.

REV. NICHOLAS UDALL, (1505-1564),

head-master at Eton, composed the first English comedy, called *Ralph Roister Doister.*

JOHN HEYWOOD, (1500-1565), a courtier, was the author of several dramatic *Interludes*, and a large collection of *Epigrams*.

MILES COVERDALE, (1488-1568), Bishop of Exeter, took part in *A Translation of the Bible*, and wrote several works against the Roman Catholic doctrines.

ROGER ASCHAM, (1515-1568), Public Orator at Cambridge, wrote a work on education entitled *The Schoolmaster*, and was celebrated for his Latin compositions.

REV. JOHN KNOX, (1505-1572), a Protestant preacher, wrote *A History of the Reformation*, and other theological works.

GEORGE GASCOIGNE, (1577), a law student, translated from Ariosto the first English prose comedy, named *The Supposes*. He was also the author of *Steel Glas*, and some other satires.

SIR PHILIP SIDNEY, (1554-1586), wrote a romance entitled *Arcadia*, several sonnets in elegant English, and *The Defence of Poesy*.

REV. JOHN FOXE, (1517-1587), an Oxford fellow, was the author of *Moralities* in Latin, and *The Book of Martyrs*, a manual of Protestantism.

ROBERT GREENE, (1553-1592), a Cambridge graduate, wrote *Friar Bacon, George a Greene*, and other plays, and some elegies and lyrics.

CHRISTOPHER MARLOWE, (1564-1593), a Cambridge graduate, wrote *Tamburlaine the Great, Doctor Faustus*, and several other sensational plays.

EDMUND SPENSER, (1552-1599), a courtier, was the author of a celebrated allegorical poem, entitled *The Faerie Queen, A View of Ireland*, and a collection of miscellaneous poetry.

RICHARD HOOKER, (1554-1600), Master of the Temple, and an eloquent preacher, is known for his work on *Ecclesiastical Polity*, defending the Church of England against the dogmatism of the Presbyterians.

JOHN STOW, (1525-1605), a tailor, was the author of a popular *Summary of English Chronicles*, and *A Survey of London*.

JOHN LYLY, (1553-1606), a courtier, wrote *Euphues, or the Anatomy of Wit*, and *Euphues and his England*, as well as several plays. He adopted an affected style which became fashionable and was called euphuism.

THOMAS SACKVILLE, EARL OF DORSET, (1536-1608), wrote several poems, and assisted in the composition of the first English tragedy, entitled *Ferrex and Porrex*, or *Gorboduc*, founded on early British legends.

FRANCIS BEAUMONT, (1586-1615), AND JOHN FLETCHER, (1576-1625), were the joint authors of more than fifty brilliant and romantic comedies and tragedies, passages from which are still frequently quoted.

WILLIAM SHAKESPEARE, (1564-1616), commenced life as an actor, and wrote thirty-seven tragedies and comedies, which hold the highest place in English literature, and have obtained an imperishable fame in every civilised country. He was also the author of several sonnets and other poems.

SIR WALTER RALEIGH, (1552-1618), wrote *A History of the World*, and some poetry.

SAMUEL DANIEL, (1562-1619), a courtier, composed a poem named *Musophilus*, several odes and sonnets, *A History of England*, and *A Defence of Rhyme*.

WILLIAM CAMDEN, (1551-1623),

head-master of Westminster School, wrote a work of considerable merit in Latin, entitled *Britannia*, giving an account of the British Isles from the earliest ages.

THOMAS LODGE, (1556-1625),

an actor, wrote several dramas, and *Rosalinde*, a novel, upon which Shakespeare founded his play of 'As You Like it.'

KING JAMES I., (1566-1625),

was the author of *Basilicon Doron*, containing advice to his son and theological arguments, and *A Counterblast to Tobacco*.

FRANCIS BACON, VISCOUNT ST. ALBANS, (1561-1626),

Lord Chancellor to James I., was a moralist, an historian, and a rhetorician, and wrote a series of philosophical and other treatises of great merit, under the general title of *Instauratio Magna*.

REV. SAMUEL
PURCHAS,
(1577-1626),

compiled, from more than thirteen hundred authors, a a work named *Pilgrimage, or the Relations of the World, the Religions observed in all Ages, and Places discovered from the Creation.*

HENRY BRIGGS,
(1556-1630),

a professor at Oxford, was the author of a series of Logarithmic Tables, entitled *Trigonometrica Britannica,* and some other valuable mathematical works.

MICHAEL DRAYTON,
(1563-1631),

an Oxford graduate, was the author of *Polyolbion,* a metrical guide-book to England and Wales, *The Battle of Agincourt,* and other historical poems, and *Nymphidia,* a fairy tale.

JOHN DONNE,
(1573-1631),

Dean of St. Paul's, wrote *The Pseudo-Martyr,* and several elegies, satires, and other poems.

EDWARD FAIRFAX, (1575-1632),

son of a baronet, translated Tasso's *Jerusalem Delivered,* and wrote a treatise on *Demonology.*

REV. GEORGE HERBERT, (1593-1632),

wrote *The Country Parson,* and some *Sacred Poems,* which are still popular.

SIR EDWARD COKE, (1552-1633),

Chief Justice to James I., was the author of *Reports and Institutes,* and other valuable legal works.

GEORGE CHAPMAN, (1557-1634),

an Oxford graduate, wrote *Eastward Ho !* a comedy depicting London life, and many other plays and poems. He also translated Homer and Hesiod.

RICHARD CORBET, (1582-1635).

Bishop of Norwich, was the author of some ludicrous *Satires* against the Puritans.

BEN JONSON, (1573-1637), was originally an actor ; he became poet - laureate, and wrote *Every Man in His Humour*, and several other plays, masques, and lyrical poems, full of vigour and fancy, but unrefined.

REV. ROBERT BURTON, (1576-1639), was the author of a well-known work, entitled *The Anatomy of Melancholy*.

PHILIP MASSINGER, (1584-1640), who was educated at Oxford, wrote *The Virgin Martyr*, and other plays, in purer taste than most of his contemporaries.

FRANCIS QUARLES, (1592-1644), a Cambridge graduate, wrote *Emblems, Divine and Moral,* and several other quaint poems and essays.

WILLIAM DRUMMOND, (1585-1649), an Edinburgh graduate, was the author of *A History of the Five Jameses,* and numerous poems, sonnets, and elegies.

JOHN SELDEN, (1584-1654),	M.P. for Oxford University, wrote *Table Talk, Titles of Honour*, and several works of great merit on constitutional and legal questions.
JOSEPH HALL, (1574-1656),	Bishop of Norwich, was the author of a book of satires, entitled *A Gathering of Rods*, and several theological treatises.
REV. THOMAS FULLER, (1608-1661),	wrote *The Worthies of England, A Church History*, and some other quaint and scholarly works.
REV. JAMES SHIRLEY, (1596-1666),	wrote *The Traitor, The Lady of Pleasure, The Cardinal*, and many other plays.
JEREMY TAYLOR, (1613-1667),	Bishop of Down, was a fluent theological writer, the titles of his best works being *Ductor Dubitantium, Holy Living, Holy Dying*, and *The Liberty of Prophesying*.

ABRAHAM COWLEY, (1618-1667),	a Cambridge graduate, was the author of a satire entitled *The Puritan and the Papist*, several poems, and translations from Anacreon.
SIR WILLIAM DAVENANT, (1605-1668),	poet-laureate, was the author of a tragedy named *Albovine*, several masques, and an epic poem entitled *Gondibert*.
SIR JOHN DENHAM, (1615-1668),	produced a successful tragedy, named *The Sophy*, and *Cooper's Hill*, a descriptive poem.
WILLIAM PRYNNE, (1600-1669),	a Puritan lawyer, wrote *Histrio Mastrix*, a virulent pamphlet against the stage, and a number of political treatises.
SIR GEORGE ETHEREDGE, (1636-1670),	was the author of *The Comical Revenge, or Love in a Tub*, some other amusing comedies, and some songs and poems.

JOHN MILTON, (1608-1674). the son of a scrivener, attained the highest rank as a poet by his *Paradise Lost* and *Paradise Regained.* He was also the author of some other poems, and several dramatic, political, and theological works.

EDWARD HYDE, EARL OF CLARENDON, (1608-1674), wrote *A History of the Rebellion,* which contains some cleverly executed descriptive portraits, and his own biography.

REV. JOHN LIGHTFOOT, (1602-1675), a celebrated Hebrew scholar, compiled *A Harmony of the Four Gospels,* and other theological works.

REV. ISAAC BARROW, (1630-1677), was the author of *Lectiones Opticæ, Lectiones Geometricæ,* and other mathematical and theological treatises.

THOMAS HOBBES, (1588-1679), Secretary to Lord Bacon, wrote *The Leviathan*, and other works on *The Science of Government*, in a very republican spirit, and on philosophical questions. He also wrote his life in Latin verse when he was eighty-five years of age.

SAMUEL BUTLER, (1612-1680), the son of a farmer, was the author of *Hudibras*, a celebrated ludicrous satire against the Puritans, full of wit and learning, and other poems.

SIR THOMAS BROWNE, (1605-1682), a physician, wrote *Religio Medici*, and other works, in a rich and impressive style, which gained him considerable reputation.

IZAAK WALTON, (1593-1683), a hosier, is known as the author of *The Complete Angler*, and some biographies.

THOMAS OTWAY, (1651-1685), an actor, wrote *Venice Preserved*, and several other coarse but thrilling plays.

SIR ROBERT FILMER, (1621-1688), a royalist, was the author of *Patriarcha*, a political essay, maintaining the divine right of kings, and that men were not born free, but slaves.

GEORGE VILLIERS, DUKE OF BUCKINGHAM, (1627-1688), was the author of a comedy entitled *The Rehearsal*, and some other plays.

JOHN BUNYAN, (1628-1688), a tinker, wrote *The Pilgrim's Progress*, a religious work, which has been translated into a greater number of languages than any other book, except the Bible.

RICHARD BAXTER, (1615-1691), a Puritan preacher, wrote *The Saints' Everlasting Rest*, and many other theological treatises.

c

SIR WILLIAM TEMPLE, (1628-1698),

a diplomatist, wrote a controversial essay on *The Comparative Merits of Ancient and Modern Authors.*

JOHN DRYDEN, (1631-1700),

poet-laureate to Charles II., was the author of numerous plays, several controversial and satirical poems, including *Absalom and Achithophel*, and many other works in verse and prose. He also made translations from *Virgil*, and some of the other Greek and Latin poets. One of his best works is *An Ode to St. Cecilia's Day.*

SAMUEL PEPYS, (1632-1703),

Secretary to the Admiralty, kept *A Diary*, which affords amusing information as to the manners and customs of the age in which he lived.

JOHN LOCKE, (1632-1704),

a country gentleman, wrote *Letters on Toleration, An*

JOHN LOCKE, (1632-1704), - continued.

Essay concerning Human Understanding, and several treatises on civil government, education, and other subjects.

JOHN EVELYN, (1620-1706),

a member of the Royal Society, was the author of *Sylva,* a discourse on forest trees, several works on the *Fine Arts,* and a *Diary* containing curious glimpses of society in the seventeenth century.

GEORGE FARQUHAR, (1678-1707),

educated at Trinity College, Dublin, became an actor, and wrote *The Beaux Stratagem,* and other plays.

CHARLES MONTAGUE, EARL OF HALIFAX, (1661-1715),

composed, jointly with Matthew Prior, a burlesque, entitled *The Country Mouse and the City Mouse,* and other poems.

GILBERT BURNET, (1643-1715),	Bishop of Salisbury, was the author of *A History of His own Time*, and other works.
REV. THOMAS PARNELL, (1679-1717),	was a contributor to periodicals, and author of a poem named *The Hermit*.
SIR SAMUEL GARTH, (1672-1718),	a physician, wrote a mock-heroic poem, entitled *The Dispensary*, and assisted in a translation of *Ovid*.
NICHOLAS ROWE, (1673-1718),	poet-laureate to George I., was the author of *Jane Shore* and other plays, a translation of *Lucan*, and a collection of poems.
JOSEPH ADDISON, (1672-1719),	Secretary of State, was an eminent essayist and the principal contributor to *The Spectator;* he was also a dramatist and poet.

MATTHEW PRIOR, (1664-1721),   a diplomatist, wrote *Henry and Emma*, and other poems, several *Tales*, and some *Epigrams*.

REV. JOSEPH BINGHAM, (1681-1723),   was the author of an interesting work entitled *Antiquities of the Christian Church*.

REV. JEREMY COLLIER, (1650-1726),   wrote an essay on the *Immorality and Profaneness of the Stage, An Ecclesiastical History*, and political pamphlets.

SIR ISAAC NEWTON, (1642-1727),   immortalised himself as the first demonstrator of *The Laws of Gravitation*, and wrote numerous scientific and philosophical treatises.

WILLIAM CONGREVE, (1670-1729),   a law student, was the author of *The Mourning Bride, The Way of the World*, and several other very successful plays.

| SIR RICHARD BLACKMORE, (1650-1729), | a physician, wrote a poem entitled *Prince Arthur*, and many others on various themes. |

SIR RICHARD STEELE, (1671-1729), contributed to three periodicals, *The Tatler*, *The Spectator*, and *The Guardian*, and was the author of several comedies and political essays.

DANIEL DEFOE, (1661-1731), a merchant, was one of the first English novelists, and his *Robinson Crusoe* is still popular. He was also a poet and political writer.

JOHN GAY, (1688-1732), a courtier, was the author of *The Beggar's Opera*, and wrote several comedies and farces, and some poems.

JOHN ARBUTHNOT, (1675-1735), a physician, wrote a humorous *History of John Bull*, and was joint author with Pope and Swift of a satirical essay entitled *Martinus Scriblerus*.

THOMAS TICKELL, (1666-1740),

an Oxford fellow, is celebrated as a translator of Homer, a contributor to *The Spectator*, and for an elegy *On the Death of Addison.*

RICHARD BENTLEY, (1662-1742),

Master of Trinity College, Cambridge, was an eminent scholar, and a critical editor of several of the *Ancient Classics.*

REV. DANIEL NEAL, (1678-1743),

a dissenting minister, wrote a reliable *History of the Puritans.*

ALEXANDER POPE, (1668-1744),

the son of a linen draper, was the author of *The Dunciad, An Essay on Man*, and many other satirical and miscellaneous poems ; he also translated *Homer.*

JONATHAN SWIFT, (1667-1745),

Dean of St. Patrick's, Dublin, was the author of numerous compositions in verse and prose, in almost every style

JONATHAN SWIFT, (1667-1745)—*continued*.

of literature. One of his best known works is *Gulliver's Travels*.

REV. ISAAC WATTS, (1674-1748),

a dissenting minister, was the author of *The Busy Bee*, *The Sluggard*, and many other hymns for children. He also wrote some theological and philosophical essays, and *A Manual of Logic*.

JAMES THOMSON, (1700-1748),

son of a Presbyterian minister, wrote a series of poems called *The Seasons*, and several tragedies.

HENRY ST. JOHN, VISCOUNT BOLINGBROKE, (1678-1751),

contributed political essays to a periodical, entitled *The Craftsman*, and wrote several metaphysical treatises.

JOSEPH BUTLER, (1692-1752),

Bishop of Durham, was the author of *The Analogy of Religion*, and many other

JOSEPH BUTLER, (1692-1752), *continued.*

very able theological works; his *Sermons on Moral Philosophy* also hold a high place in Church literature.

GEORGE BERKELEY, (1684-1753)

Bishop of Cloyne, wrote *A Treatise on the Principles of Human Knowledge*, a theological dialogue entitled *Alciphron*, and several very able political and metaphysical works.

HENRY FIELDING, (1707-1754),

educated for the law, was the author of *Tom Jones, Joseph Andrews*, and other novels of great merit; he also wrote plays and political pamphlets.

WILLIAM COLLINS, (1721-1756),

the son of a hatter, was the author of *An Ode to the Passions*, and some other poems.

COLLEY CIBBER, (1671-1757), an actor and poet-laureate, wrote *The Careless Husband* and several other plays, and *An Apology for his Life.*

ALLAN RAMSAY, (1686-1758), a bookseller, wrote *The Vision*, *The Gentle Shepherd*, and several collections of miscellaneous poems.

REV. JOHN DYER, (1700-1758), was the author of *Grongar Hill*, and other descriptive poems.

SAMUEL RICHARDSON, (1689-1761), a printer, was the author of three celebrated novels, entitled *Pamela, Clarissa Harlowe*, and *Sir Charles Grandison.*

LADY MARY WORTLEY MONTAGU, (1689-1762), wrote several poems, and described her *Travels in the East* in a series of letters which are still read with pleasure.

WILLIAM SHENSTONE, an Oxford student, wrote *The* (1714-1763), *Schoolmistress*, and several odes and elegies.

REV. EDWARD was the author of *Night* YOUNG, *Thoughts*, several satires, and (1681-1765), three tragedies.

REV. CHARLES was the author of *The Rosciad*, CHURCHILL, a satire on the stage, and (1731-1765), various other poems.

REV. LAURENCE wrote two humorous narratives, STERNE, entitled *Tristram Shandy* and (1713-1768), *A Sentimental Journey*, and some satires.

JAMES MERRICK, fellow of Trinity College, Ox- (1720-1769), ford, was the author of *The Chameleon*, and several theo- logical works.

WILLIAM FALCONER, a naval officer, was the author (1732-1769), of *The Shipwreck*, a vivid descriptive poem.

MARK AKENSIDE, a physician, wrote *The Pleas-*
(1721-1770), *ures of Imagination*, a poem
of much merit.

THOMAS CHATTERTON, the son of a sexton, composed
(1752-1770), imaginary *Legendary Histories*,
and miscellaneous poems, un-
equalled by any writer of his
age.

THOMAS GRAY, a professor at Cambridge, was
(1716-1771), the author of the famous
Elegy in a Country Church-
yard, and several odes.

TOBIAS SMOLLETT, a naval surgeon, wrote *Roderick*
(1721-1771), *Random, Peregrine Pickle,*
Humphrey Clinker, and some
other satirical novels.

PHILIP STANHOPE, wrote a series of *Letters to His*
EARL OF CHESTERFIELD, *Son*, full of practical sense and
(1694-1773), useful information.

OLIVER GOLDSMITH, (1728-1774),
a medical student, was the author of *The Vicar of Wakefield*, several poems, a play entitled *She Stoops to Conquer*, and some historical works.

DAVID HUME, (1711-1776),
Under-Secretary of State, compiled *A History of England*, and wrote several political and metaphysical treatises.

JOHN ARMSTRONG, (1709-1779),
a physician, was the author of *The Art of Preserving Health*, one of the finest didactic poems ever written.

SAMUEL JOHNSON, (1709-1784),
the son of a bookseller, compiled a *Dictionary*, and wrote *The Lives of the Poets*, a tragedy, a novel, and essays on various subjects.

SIR WILLIAM BLACKSTONE, (1723-1784),
an eminent judge, was the author of a well-known work, entitled *Commentaries on the Laws of England*.

ADAM SMITH, (1723-1790),

a professor at Glasgow University, was the author of *The Wealth of Nations*, a treatise on political economy.

THOMAS WARTON, (1728-1790),

poet-laureate, wrote *A History of English Poetry*, and several other works.

REV. JOHN WESLEY, (1703-1791),

was the author of a *Journal*, a translation of *The Works of Thomas à Kempis*, a German divine, several hymns, and some theological treatises.

SIR JOSHUA REYNOLDS, (1723-1792),

a painter, wrote *Discourses on Painting*, and *Remarks on Pictures of the Dutch and Flemish Schools.*

REV. GILBERT WHITE, (1720-1793),

a celebrated naturalist, was the author of *The Natural History and Antiquities of Selborne.*

EDWARD GIBBON, (1737-1794), the son of a country gentleman, devoted many years to a history of *The Decline and Fall of the Roman Empire*, which has been translated into almost every European language, and an autobiography.

JAMES BOSWELL, (1740-1795), a Scotch advocate, was a companion of Dr. Johnson, whose biography he wrote.

JAMES MACPHERSON, (1738-1796), a Scotch schoolmaster, translated several of the ancient Gaelic poems of *Ossian*.

ROBERT BURNS, (1759-1796), a Scotch farmer, was the author of *The Cottar's Saturday Night, John Anderson my Jo, Auld Lang Syne*, and many other sentimental and patriotic songs, as popular now as when they were written.

HORACE WALPOLE, (1717-1797),

M.P., was the author of a novel entitled *The Castle of Otranto, Anecdotes of Painters*, and several other works; he was also celebrated as a letter-writer.

EDMUND BURKE, (1728-1797),

M.P. for Wendover, wrote *Essays* on various social and political subjects: but his fame rests upon his eloquent speeches in Parliament.

WILLIAM COWPER, (1731-1800),

a barrister, was the author of *The Task*, several other poems and moral satires, and the humorous *History of John Gilpin*.

JAMES BEATTIE, (1735-1803),

a professor at Aberdeen, wrote *Essays on Moral Science*, a poem entitled *The Minstrel*, and several other works.

REV. WILLIAM PALEY, was the author of *The Ele-*
(1743-1805), *ments of Moral and Political Philosophy*, *The Evidences of Christianity*, and other theological works ; he was also a translator of the Classics.

HENRY KIRKE WHITE, of humble origin, wrote *Mis-*
(1785-1806), *cellaneous Poems* of considerable merit.

REV. JOHN HOME, a Scotch minister, was the
(1722-1808), author of a clever tragedy named *Douglas*, for writing which he had to retire from his kirk.

RICHARD PORSON, a professor at Cambridge, was
(1759-1808), an eminent Greek scholar and critic, and edited four plays of *Euripides*.

CHARLES DIBDIN, a musician, wrote *Poor Jack*,
(1745-1814), and many other favourite ballads and sea songs.

D

RICHARD BRINSLEY SHERIDAN, (1751-1817),   an Under-Secretary of State, wrote three celebrated plays, entitled *The Rivals, The School for Scandal,* and *The Critic ;* and made some brilliant speeches in Parliament.

JANE AUSTEN, (1775-1817),   a clergyman's daughter, was the authoress of *Pride and Prejudice, Sense and Sensibility,* and several other popular domestic novels.

SIR PHILIP FRANCIS, (1740-1818),   was the reputed author of a series of pungent political letters signed *Junius.*

JOHN KEATS, (1795-1821),   educated for the medical profession, wrote *Endymion, An Ode to a Nightingale, Hyperion,* and many other elegant poems.

PERCY BYSSHE SHELLEY, (1792-1822),	eldest son of a baronet, was a gifted writer with extreme revolutionary ideas. His best poetical works are *Prometheus Unbound*, and *The Cenci ;* he was also the author of several romances, and translations from the Greek Classics.
THOMAS ERSKINE, (1750-1823),	Lord Chancellor to George III., was the author of several political pamphlets.
ANN RADCLIFFE, (1764-1823),	wife of a journalist, wrote *The Romance of the Forest, The Mysteries of Udolpho,* and several other thrilling novels.
MRS. BARBAULD, (1743-1824),	was a well-known writer of *Poems and Hymns for Children.*
LORD BYRON, (1788-1824),	was a poet of extraordinary genius, power, and versatility ; two of his most popular works being *Childe Harold* and *Don Juan.*

WILLIAM GIFFORD, (1756-1826),

of humble origin, became editor of *The Quarterly Review*, and wrote successful satires against the Italian style of poetry and the modern drama.

REGINALD HEBER, (1783-1826),

Bishop of Calcutta, was the author of a favourite collection of *Hymns* and *Sacred Poems*.

WILLIAM MITFORD, (1744-1827),

M.P., devoted many years to a *History of Greece*.

GEORGE CANNING, (1770-1827),

Prime Minister, contributed in his earlier days to the *Anti-Jacobin*, a satirical periodical.

REV. DR. LANIGAN, (1760-1828),

was the author of a calm and learned *Ecclesiastical History of Ireland*.

SIR HUMPHREY DAVY, (1778-1829),

President of the Royal Society, wrote numerous treatises on *Physical Science and Chemical Philosophy*.

WILLIAM HAZLITT, (1778-1830), son of a Unitarian minister, was an eminent critic and essayist, and the author of *Sketches of English Picture Galleries*, and various other works.

THOMAS HOPE, (1770-1831), an architect, was the author of a novel entitled *Anastatius or The Memoirs of a Modern Greek*, and essays on *Architecture* and *Household Furniture*.

REV. GEORGE CRABBE, (1754-1832), wrote *The Library*, *Tales of the Hall*, and other narrative poems.

SIR WALTER SCOTT, (1771-1832), was the prince of novelists, and the author of numerous romantic poems and ballads; he also contributed to the *Edinburgh* and *Quarterly Reviews*.

JEREMY BENTHAM, (1748-1832),	a barrister, wrote *The Principles of Morals and Legislation*, and other utilitarian treatises.
HANNAH MORE, (1745-1833),	was a writer of *Sacred Dramas* and other popular works.
SAMUEL TAYLOR COLERIDGE, (1772-1834),	the son of a clergyman, became a poet, a critic, and a metaphysician ; his best works being *The Ancient Mariner*, *Christabel*, and *Aids to Reflection*.
CHARLES LAMB, (1775-1834),	a clerk in the India Office, was the author of *Essays of Elia*, a clever series of humorous sketches, and *Tales from Shakespeare*.
WILLIAM COBBETT, (1762-1835),	a self-educated farmer, was the editor of *The Weekly Register*, a domestic journal, and the author of some educational and political publications.

James Hogg, (1772-1835),	known as the Ettrick Shepherd, was the author of several collections of songs and ballads, of which the finest are *The Queen's Wake* and *The Skylark*.
Mrs. Hemans, (1793-1835),	wrote *Songs of the Affections*, *Lays of Many Lands*, and various miscellaneous poems.
James Mill, (1773-1836),	was educated for the Scotch Kirk, but preferred literature. He wrote a *History of British India*, and several works on political economy and philosophical subjects.
L. E. Landon, (Mrs. M'Lean), (1802-1839),	contributed poetry to several periodicals. She also wrote *The Fate of Adelaide* a Swiss tale, and three novels.

FANNY BURNEY, (MADAME D'ARBLAY), (1752-1840), waiting woman to Queen Charlotte, wrote *Evelina* and some other clever novels. She has also recorded her experience at Court in her *Diary* and *Letters*.

THEODORE HOOK, (1788-1841), an Oxford graduate, could improvise on any subject, and was the author of *Jack Brag*, *Maxwell*, and other novels, besides numerous satirical and humorous essays and sketches.

ALLAN CUNNINGHAM, (1784-1842), of humble origin, wrote novels, poems, a drama, biographies, and numerous Scottish songs and ballads.

REV. THOMAS ARNOLD, (1795-1842), head-master of Rugby School, wrote a *History of Rome*, and *Lectures on Modern History*.

Robert Southey, (1774-1843), poet-laureate, was the author of *Thalaba, The Curse of Kehama,* and other poems, *The Doctor,* numerous translations from Spanish and Portuguese writers, and several biographies, ; he also contributed to the *Quarterly Review.*

Thomas Campbell, (1777-1844), son of a merchant, established his fame as a poet by his *Pleasures of Hope,* and wrote several other poems of considerable merit.

Rev. Richard Barham, (1780-1845), was the author of *The Ingoldsby Legends,* a series of humorous tales in verse.

Thomas Hood, (1799-1845), son of a bookseller, wrote *The Bridge of Sighs, Eugene Aram, The Song of a Shirt,* and many other pathetic and humorous poems ; he also edited a *Comic Annual,* and contributed to several magazines.

LADY NAIRNE, (1766-1845), was the authoress of *Caller Herrin'*, *The Laird of Cockpen*, *Lays from Strathearn*, and other popular lyrical poetry.

ISAAC D'ISRAELI, (1766-1848), son of a retired merchant, wrote *The Curiosities of Literature*, and other works on the same subject.

MARIA EDGEWORTH, (1767-1849), the daughter of a mechanical engineer, was the authoress of *Belinda*, and many other admirable tales of Irish life.

COUNTESS OF BLESSINGTON, (1789-1849), wrote her *Conversations with Byron*, and several novels, travels, sketches, and memoirs.

HARTLEY COLERIDGE, (1796-1849), an Oxford scholar, contributed to *Blackwood* and other magazines; he also wrote *The Lives of Northern Worthies*, and *The Life of Massinger*, a dramatist.

CAPTAIN MARRYAT, (1797-1849),	R.N., wrote *Midshipman Easy*, *Peter Simple*, *Jacob Faithful*, and many other naval novels.
WILLIAM WORDSWORTH, (1770-1850),	poet-laureate, was the author of *The Excursion*, and numerous other poems of great beauty.
LORD JEFFREY, (1773-1850),	a Scotch judge, was the first editor of the *Edinburgh Review*, and wrote several clever critical essays.
JOANNA BAILLIE, (1762-1851),	the daughter of a Presbyterian minister, wrote a series of *Plays on the Passions*, and some miscellaneous poetry.
DR. JOHN LINGARD, (1771-1851),	of humble origin, wrote a lucid and impartial *History of England*, and some theological treatises.
THOMAS MOORE, (1779-1852),	educated for the law, was the author of *Irish Melodies*, *Lalla Rookh*, and many other works.

AMELIA OPIE,   wrote *Tales of Real Life*, and
(1769-1853),   some poems.

JAMES MONTGOMERY,   of humble origin, wrote *The
(1771-1854),   Wanderer in Switzerland*, and
                    other descriptive and mis-
                    cellaneous poetry.

JOHN WILSON,   a Scotch advocate, contributed
(CHRISTOPHER NORTH), *Noctes Ambrosianæ* to *Black-
(1785-1854),   wood's Magazine*, and wrote
                    several tales and essays.

SAMUEL ROGERS,   a banker, wrote *The Pleasures
(1763-1855),   of Memory*, and other poems.

CHARLOTTE BRONTE,   a clergyman's daughter, wrote
(CURRER BELL),   *Jane Eyre*, a work of great
(1816-1855),   genius, and several other
                    novels.

SIR WILLIAM   a celebrated Scotch meta-
HAMILTON,   physician, contributed to the
(1791-1856),   *Edinburgh Review*, and wrote
                    treatises on logic and mental
                    philosophy.

DOUGLAS JERROLD, (1803-1857),   the son of a theatrical manager, was the author of *Black-eyed Susan* and other plays, *Mrs. Caudle's Lectures*, and numerous other sparkling and satirical compositions. He was also a journalist.

HENRY HALLAM, (1777-1859),   an Oxford graduate, was the author of a *Constitutional History of England*, and an *Introduction to the Literature of Europe*, both of which evince great industry, acuteness, and impartiality.

LORD MACAULAY, (1800-1859),   wrote. *The Lays of Ancient Rome*, a *History of England*, and numerous other poems and essays. He also contributed to several periodicals, and for brilliancy of style, and elegant diction, holds the highest rank among English writers.

J. H. LEIGH HUNT, (1784-1859),	the son of a solicitor, was a poet and essayist, the editor of the *London Journal*, and the author of various works in prose and verse.
THOMAS DE QUINCEY, (1785-1859),	the son of a merchant, was the author of *Confessions of an Opium Eater*, and an impassioned and critical writer in several periodicals.
GENERAL SIR WILLIAM NAPIER, (1785-1860),	wrote a *History of the Peninsular War*, and other works on India.
G. P. R. JAMES, (1801-1860),	was the author of *Richelieu, De Lorne*, and many other historical romances.
LORD CAMPBELL, (1781-1861),	Lord Chancellor, was the author of a series of *The Lives of the Lord Chancellors*, and another of *The Chief Justices of England*.

Mrs. Browning, (1809-1861),	was the highly-educated and talented authoress of *Seraphim*, *Aurora Leigh*, and several other poems.
Sir Francis Palgrave, (1788-1861),	wrote *The Merchant and the Friar*, and other works, evincing antiquarian and medieval knowledge and research.
J. Sheridan Knowles, (1784-1862),	an actor, produced *The Hunchback*, *Love Chase*, and some other plays.
William Makepeace Thackeray, (1811-1863),	the son of an Indian civil servant, contributed to *Punch* and several magazines, and earned great reputation as the author of *Vanity Fair*, *Pendennis*, and several other novels, and as a lecturer on *English Humourists*, and *The Four Georges*.

MRS. TROLLOPE,   was the authoress of *Travels*
(1779-1863),   *in America*, and numerous
                     novels.

RICHARD WHATELY,   Archbishop of Dublin, wrote
(1787-1863),   several valuable works on
                     Logic and *Rhetoric*.

SIR GEORGE   a statesman, was the author
CORNEWALL LEWIS,   of numerous essays on science,
(1806-1863),   history, and philosophy. He
                     also conducted the *Edinburgh
                     Review*.

WALTER SAVAGE   having squandered his estate,
LANDOR,   became an author, and wrote
(1775-1864),   *Imaginary   Conversations*,
                     which are full of scholarship
                     and humour, as well as poems
                     and essays.

CHARLES WENT-   a civil servant, became a well-
WORTH DILKE,   known critic and journalist,
(1789-1864),   and wrote essays on literary
                     history.

REV. JOHN KEBLE, (1792-1865), was the author of *The Christian Year*, and several theological works.

MRS. GASKELL, (1822-1865), the wife of a Unitarian minister, wrote *Mary Barton*, and other novels depicting artisan life.

WILLIAM AYTOUN, (1813-1865), a graduate of Edinburgh, was the author of *The Execution of Montrose, Lays of the Scottish Cavaliers*, and several humorous ballads. He also contributed to *Blackwood's Magazine*.

REV. WILLIAM WHEWELL, (1794-1867), was an eminent writer on mathematics, science, philosophy, and other subjects.

MICHAEL FARADAY, (1791-1867), of humble origin, attained great eminence as a lecturer and writer on *Chemistry* and *Electricity*.

E.

SIR ARCHIBALD
ALISON,
(1792-1867),

devoted many years to the compilation of *A History of Europe*, which has a world-wide popularity.

HENRY BROUGHAM,
(1778-1868),

Lord Chancellor, achieved a great reputation as an orator, and was a contributor to the *Edinburgh Review*, and the author of several works on theology, science, and meta-physics.

SIR DAVID BREWSTER,
(1781-1868),

devoted his life to science, and wrote numerous treatises on *Light* and *Optics*.

HENRY HART
MILMAN,
(1791-1868),

Dean of St. Paul's, was the author of *Fazio*, a tragedy, *The Fall of Jerusalem*, *A History of Latin Christianity*, and many other historical and theological works.

SAMUEL LOVER, (1797-1868),	originally a miniature painter, was a celebrated Irish novelist and song writer. *Handy Andy*, *Rory O'More*, and *Molly Bawn*, are some of his best compositions.
WILLIAM CARLETON, (1798-1869),	of humble origin, wrote *Traits and Stories of the Irish Peasantry*, and other humorous and pathetic tales.
CHARLES DICKENS, (1812-1870),	the son of a civil servant, was the author of *The Pickwick Papers*, a series of popular novels, and several *Christmas Stories*, chiefly delineating the life of the masses. He was also the editor of a periodical entitled *Household Words*.
SIR JOHN HERSCHEL, (1792-1871),	wrote many treatises on *Astronomy*, and other scientifi subjects.

SIR RODERICK MURCHISON, (1792-1871),	was President of the Geographical Society, and the author of several works on *Geology*.
GEORGE GROTE, (1794-1871),	a banker, wrote a most valuable *History of Greece*, and a number of political pamphlets.
AUGUSTUS DE MORGAN, (1806 1871).	a Cambridge wrangler, was the author of a *Treatise on the Differential and Integral Calculus*, and many other mathematical works. He also published an amusing *Budget of Paradoxes*.
HENRY ALFORD, (1810-1871),	Dean of Canterbury, wrote *The School of the Heart*, and other poems, and was an eminent Greek scholar.
REV. FREDERICK DENISON MAURICE, (1806-1872),	the son of a Unitarian minister, was the author of *Mental and Moral Philosophy*,

Rev. Frederick Denison Maurice, (1806-1872)— *continued.*	and several theological treatises inculcating Broad Church doctrines.
Charles James Lever, (1806-1872),	a physician, wrote *Harry Lorrequer, Charles O'Malley, Jack Hinton,* and many other brilliantly humorous Irish novels.
Mrs. Somerville, (1780-1873),	was the authoress of *The Connexion of the Physical Sciences, Physical Geography,* and other popular scientific works.
Charles Knight, (1791-1873),	the son of a bookseller, was a Shakespearian commentator, and the publisher of *The Penny Cyclopædia,* and a variety of cheap and instructive literature.
John Stuart Mill, (1806-1873),	M.P., was the author of numerous works on *Political Economy,* with a strong democratic and agnostic bias.

LORD LYTTON, (1806-1873), was a richly gifted and versatile writer of plays, romances, and novels. *The Lady of Lyons* and *Money* are his best dramas, and *The Last Days of Pompeii*, *Rienzi*, and *The Pilgrims of the Rhine*, his most popular fictions.

CHARLES SHIRLEY BROOKS, (1816-1874), the son of an architect, was a journalist and play-writer, but is best known as a contributor to *Punch*.

BRYAN WALLER PROCTER, (BARRY CORNWALL), (1787-1874), educated for the law, wrote a number of miscellaneous poems, and several biographies.

CONNOP THIRLWALL, (1797-1875), Bishop of St. David's, was an able literary and theological writer, and an advocate for religious toleration.

SIR CHARLES LYELL, (1797-1875), was the author of several valuable works on *Geology*.

LORD MAHON, (EARL STANHOPE), (1805-1875), wrote *A History of England, A Life of Belisarius*, and several essays and biographies.

HON. MRS. NORTON, (LADY STIRLING MAXWELL), (1808-1875), was a sentimental ballad writer, and the authoress of *Stuart of Dunleath, Lost and Saved*, and other novels.

REV. CHARLES KINGSLEY, (1819-1875), wrote several poems, and was the author of *Alton Locke, Yeast*, and other novels, evincing strong sympathy with the working classes.

JOHN FORSTER, (1812-1876), a barrister, was an eminent journalist, and the biographer of Goldsmith, Dickens, Swift, and other men of note.

HARRIET MARTINEAU, (1802-1876), descended from a Huguenot family, was the authoress of *Illustrations of Political Economy*, some *Historical Works* and *Travels*, and biographical notices.

SAMUEL WARREN, (1807-1877), a barrister, wrote *The Diary of a Late Physician, Ten Thousand a Year*, and some other sensational novels.

WILLIAM HEPWORTH DIXON, (1821-1879), a barrister, was the author of *New America, Free Russia, The Switzers*, and other historical and biographical works.

TOM TAYLOR, (1817-1880), a civil servant, wrote *The Ticket of Leave Man, Masks and Faces, 'Twixt Axe and Crown*, and upwards of a hundred other plays.

George Eliot, (Mary Ann Evans). (1820-1880), was the authoress of *Scenes of Clerical Life*, several poems and essays, *Adam Bede*, *Silas Marner*, *Middlemarch*, *Daniel Deronda*, and other novels, all evincing rare genius and knowledge of human nature.

Thomas Carlyle, (1795-1881), the son of a Scotch mason, was a stern censor of the age he lived in, a contributor to several magazines, and the author of *Sartor Resartus, A History of Frederick the Great*, and many other historical and philosophical works.

Benjamin D'Israeli, Earl of Beaconsfield, (1804-1881), commenced his success as a political novelist with *Vivian Grey*, and crowned it with *Endymion*.

John Hill Burton, (1809-1881), a barrister, wrote *A History of Scotland*, and on political economy.

ARTHUR PENRHYN STANLEY, (1815-1881),	Dean of Westminster, was the author of *Travels in Palestine*, the *Life of Dr. Arnold*, and other works.
REV. EDWARD B. PUSEY, (1800-1882),	an Oxford professor, was a contributor to *Tracts for the Times*, and the author of numerous works advocating High Church doctrines.
WILLIAM HARRISON AINSWORTH, (1805-1882),	a journalist, wrote *Jack Shepherd*, *The Tower of London*, and some other popular but pernicious novels.
CHARLES DARWIN, (1809-1882),	a graduate of Cambridge, became famous as a naturalist and physiologist, and was the author of *The Origin of the Species*, *The Descent of Man*, and several scientific works.

ANTHONY TROLLOPE, (1815-1883),	a civil servant, will be remembered as the author of *Dr. Thorne*, *Framley Parsonage*, *Barchester Towers*, and many other amusing novels, and books of travel, and of his own biography.

ROBERT AND WILLIAM CHAMBERS, (1802-1871), (1800-1883),	the sons of a Scotch weaver, were the eminent publishers of the *Edinburgh Journal*, *A History of English Literature*, and many educational works of great merit.

REV. GEORGE POOLE, (1810-1883),	was the author of *A History of Ecclesiastical Architecture in England*, and other works.

JOHN WILLIAM COLENSO, (1814-1883),	Bishop of Natal, was the author of some useful *Mathematical* works, and of *Commentaries on The Pentateuch*

JOHN WILLIAM COLENSO, (1814-1883) *continued.*

and Book of Joshua, of great ability but questionable orthodoxy.

WILLIAM SPOTTISWOODE, (1825-1883),

an Oxford scholar, and printer to the Queen, wrote a treatise on the *Polarisation of Light*, and various works on philosophy, astronomy, popular education, and other subjects.

JOHN PAYNE COLLIER, (1789-1883),

a barrister, was a Shakespearian critic, and the author of *The Poetical Decameron, The Poet's Pilgrimage*, and *A Bibliographical Catalogue*.

HENRY WADSWORTH LONGFELLOW, (1807-1882),

No record of writers in the English language would be complete which did not include the author of *Hyperion, Kavanagh, The Song of Hia-*

HENRY WADSWORTH LONGFELLOW, (1807-1882)— *continued*. — *watha*, and many other works which are as popular with English readers as with his own countrymen in America, and breathe a spirit of love and purity unsurpassed in the literature of any other nation, either ancient or modern.

DINAH MARIA MULOCK, (1827-1887), authoress of *John Halifax, Gentleman*, and several other clever novels.

MRS. HENRY WOOD, (1821-1887), authoress of *East Lynne*, and numerous other sensational novels, which have attained an aggregate sale of half-a-million copies.

MATTHEW ARNOLD, (1822-1888), professor of poetry at Oxford, and a writer on religious, social, and educational subjects.

WILKIE COLLINS,   a celebrated novelist; author
(1824-1889),   of *After Dark, A Woman in
                    White, No Name*, and many
                    other works.

ELIZA COOK,   authoress of *The Old Arm
(1819-1889),   Chair*, and numerous other
                    poems and prose works in
                    various periodicals.

ROBERT BROWNING,   a prolific writer of poetry, and
(1813-1890),   the author of several plays.

DION BOUCICAULT,   a dramatist and actor; author
(1823-1890),   of *London Assurance, Colleen
                    Bawn, Arrah na Pogue*, and
                    several other plays.

LORD TENNYSON,   the most distinguished of
(1809-1892),   modern British poets; was
                    appointed Poet Laureate in
                    1850. *The Princess* and *In
                    Memoriam* are two of his
                    best known works.

WALT WHITMAN, (1819-1892),	an American, celebrated for his unconventional poems, the best being *Leaves of Grass*, and *Democratic Vistas*.
JAMES ANTHONY FROUDE, (1818-1894),	professor of modern history at Oxford; author of numerous works including a wide range of literature.
EDMUND YATES, (1831-1894),	an able critic, journalist, and novel writer, and the founder of *The World* newspaper.
GEORGE DU MAURIER, (1834-1896),	a celebrated contributor to *Punch*, and a book illustrator.
HARRIET BEECHER STOWE, (1812-1896),	the famous American authoress of *Uncle Tom's Cabin*, and other works.
MRS. MARGARET OLIPHANT, (1828-1897),	a writer of novels and histories, equally remarkable for their high standard, and the amount of work which she succeeded in accomplishing.

THE BIRD'S COMMENTS.

THE TRAVELLER who gazes, from an eminence, on the bird's-eye view which it affords of a newly-visited city or locality, is glad to have his attention directed to the principal objects of interest in the somewhat confusing expanse around him : and readers of the foregoing Synopsis will probably be better able to retain its impression on their mental vision with the aid of a few general observations upon some of the chief points, concerning which it is intended to create a desire for further information.

The gift of language enabled mankind, from the earliest ages, to communicate their thoughts and ideas to each other : and, long before the invention of writing, songs were composed by the bards or priests in every civilised country, to be recited at their religious ceremonies, or to kindle courage in battle. These were orally handed down from generation to generation, and formed the main source of all subsequent historical records and other literature.

It must also be remembered, in connection with the rise and progress of English learning, that, for centuries prior to the Christian era, intellectual culture had attained its highest development in ancient Greece and Rome, and that from the writings of the celebrated authors of those days,— whose works were almost miraculously preserved during the dark ages which followed the downfall of the Roman Empire,—all that is most valuable in our secular knowledge and literature, except a fuller acquaintance with the laws of nature, has been derived.

The Angles are supposed to have brought with them to Britain, in the fifth century, a composition in praise of the deeds of their ancestors, called "The Gleeman's Song," which, with two others, entitled "The Battle of Finsburgh" and "The Tale of Beowulf," were afterwards committed to writing, and constitute the only specimens of their language and poetry.

Caedmon was a native of Britain, and therefore

F

heads the roll of Anglo - Saxon writers. Bede, and several of his successors, wrote in Latin, because that language was adopted by the monks as better suited than the rude vernacular for literary purposes. King Alfred, however, endeavoured to instruct his people by means of translations : but his example does not seem to have been followed, the writers during the next two centuries having chiefly devoted themselves to historical annals and controversial theology. The earliest dawn of romance was the engrafting into their works, by Mapes and others, in the twelfth century, of the Welsh legends relating to King Arthur. The first work on English law appeared soon afterwards, and Roger Bacon's treatises on science and general knowledge a century later. Satire and criticism followed next, and the Anglo-Saxon language, which was gradually changing into Norman-English, began to be used more generally than Latin.

During the fourteenth century vice and misery were depicted in allegorical poetry, and the spirit of inquiry was stimulated by travels and philosophical disquisitions. Wycliffe's translation of the Bible helped, at the same time, to enforce the doctrines of the religious reformers, and Chaucer's poetry awakened an interest in human character and daily life.

The wars of the Roses caused a decadence of literature during the fifteenth century; but a revival ensued, and translations from the ancient classics, as well as sonnets and love songs imitated from Italian poetry, considerably expanded the range of thought, and imparted a more elegant tone to the language. Miracle plays representing scriptural events, which had been originated soon after the introduction of Christianity, were superseded by comedies and tragedies, and romances in verse and prose became popular.

In the sixteenth century the diffusion of knowledge by means of the printing-press, the discovery of new countries, and the spread of the Reformation, all tended to kindle imagination, and to enlarge the intellectual ideas of the nation generally. The Elizabethan dramas, culminating with those of Shakespeare, have never been excelled in their grandeur and variety, their perfect delineations of human nature, their wealth of incident, or their exuberance of wit. The poetry of the period also, whether descriptive, satirical, or humorous, bore the impress of developed power and refinement; while the prose compositions, in almost every branch of learning, attained a depth of tone, and a classic grace of style, which have served as models to many subsequent writers. Lord Bacon rivalled his earlier namesake in his philosophical and scientific attainments, and Spenser's pastoral and allegorical poems were succeeded by those of Milton.

The civil war in the seventeenth century again almost silenced the voice of literature, with the exception of political treatises, and Puritanical rule suppressed the drama. In the reaction that followed the Restoration, a new style, borrowed from the French, which was characterised by degrading coarseness and scoffing ridicule, prevailed for a time.

During the first half of the eighteenth century, which is known as the English "Augustan" age, the poetical compositions, although perfect in metre, were deficient in passion and grace. The style of the chief prose writers, however, was simple and vigorous. In the next generation several of the noblest specimens of English writing were produced, and the poetry became more fervid and natural. Works of fiction took the place of tragedies and comedies, while history, science, and philosophy were more generally studied and popularised. The newspaper press and periodical criticism became, from this time, powerful influences in guiding public opinion, and satire the keenest weapon for assailing the vices both of the rich and poor.

The stirring incidents of the first French Revolution gave birth to an entirely new development of mental activity, which is still perceptible in the greater freedom of thought, and in the widened scope of the literature of the nineteenth century. More practical than that of any preceding age, it at the same time indicates an intellectual energy, and (excepting the effusions of sensational novelists) a moral pureness, which should earn for the writers of the Victorian era, including many who are still living, an enduring fame in the estimation of posterity.

INDEX.

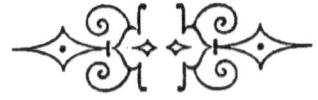

William Byles & Sons, Printers, 129, Fleet Street, London, and Bradford.

NEW EDITION.

THE CLASSICS
FOR THE MILLION:

BEING

AN EPITOME,

IN ENGLISH,

OF THE WORKS OF

THE PRINCIPAL GREEK AND LATIN AUTHORS

BY

HENRY GREY.

EIGHTEENTH THOUSAND.

OPINIONS OF THE PRESS.

' Mr. Grey displays the art of condensation in a scholarly manner throughout his work.'—*Clifton Chronicle.*

' Gives the very essence of the ancient authors.'—*Dorset County Chronicle.*

' The result of much reading, labour, and thought.'—*Druids' Journal.*

' Accomplished in a masterly and scholarly manner.'—*Ecclesiastical Gazette.*

' A most useful and instructive work.'—*Edinburgh Courant.*

' Will make the reader in a very brief time acquainted with the Classics ; the quotations are well selected.'—*Evangelical Magazine.*

' Supplies a manifest want.'—*Glasgow Herald.*

' A compact handbook to all that is best in the ancient Classics.'—*Harper's New Monthly Magazine.*

' It is astonishing how much is done in a pleasant, chatty manner ; the book will certainly afford pleasure.'—*Illustrated London News.*

' A most interesting and complete work.'—*Jewish World.*

' An admirable *résumé*, and a good introductory guide for school-boys.'—*John Bull.*

' Very few possess the power of analysis and condensation exhibited in this useful manual.'—*Life.*

' We have never seen such scholarly work at so low a price.'—*Lincoln Gazette.*

' A wonderful *multum in parvo.'—Literary Churchman.*

' Will be of use to those who are making acquaintance with authors of whose works they too often fail to acquire any general idea.'—*Literary World.*

' The work of condensation is done in a skilful and scholarly manner.' —*Manchester Courier.*

' An absorbingly interesting work.'—*Marlborough Times.*

' A marvel of condensation and cheapness.'—*Melbourne Portfolio.*

' A very readable book.'—*Modern Society.*

' Exactly the kind of book needed in this busy age.'—*Montreal Gazette.*

' Imparts knowledge which it would take years to acquire from the books themselves.'—*Montrose Standard.*

' Suitable for hose leaving elementary schols, as well as for students.' —*Newport Advertiser.*

' Very well done.'—*New York Nation.*

' A model of careful composition, and a treasure to those who are unable to study the Classics more fully.'—*North British Daily Mail.*

'Gives the striking features of each author with clear incisiveness.'—*Otago Times.*

'Whether for educational purposes, or for ordinary reading, it has no rival.'—*Oxford Chronicle.*

'An excellent idea.' — *Oxford and Cambridge Undergraduates' Journal.*

'Will certainly excite a taste for the Classics.'—*People's Journal, Dundee.*

'We discern indications of highly educated power.'—*Public Opinion.*

'A well-prepared biographical, critical, and explanatory epitome.'—*Quebec Chronicle.*

'The idea is a good one, and exceedingly well carried out.'—*Rock.*

'Mr. Grey has performed his laborious task with considerable tact and skill.'—*School Guardian.*

'The work is done with much conscientiousness.'—*Scotsman.*

'Of great use for elder boys and girls.'—*Scottish Guardian.*

'Worthy of all praise.'—*Sligo Chronicle.*

'Mr. Grey has done much towards familiarising the masses with the grandeur of ancient learning.'—*Society.*

'An excellent work, written with thorough appreciation of the essentials in literature.'—*St. Andrew's Gazette.*

'Well compressed, and yet retaining a sprightliness of manner rather rare in such works.'—*Sword and Trowel.*

'The story, the satire, or the moral is concisely told in excellently chosen words.'—*Sydney Telegraph.*

'Exactly what a classical student needs.'—*Tablet.*

'Mr. Grey has executed his task well and judiciously.'—*Times.*

'A great success.'—*Toronto Mail.*

'Invaluable for obtaining a general idea of each author.'—*Whitehall Review.*

'Mr. Grey writes with the ease that comes from intimate acquaintance with his subject.'—*Wilts and Gloucestershire Standard.*

'Evinces great research and ability, and opens up a wide field of instruction and entertainment.'—*Windsor and Eton Gazette.*

'Mr. Grey possesses the talent of compression in a very high degree.'—*World.*

'It fills a gap in literature, and everything objectionable has been omitted.'—*Y. Great, Welsh Review.*

'A pleasant reminder, an encouraging help, and a boon to those whose reading time is limited.'—*Yorkshire Post.*

NEW EDITION.

A KEY TO
THE WAVERLEY NOVELS,

IN CHRONOLOGICAL SEQUENCE,

WITH INDEX OF THE PRINCIPAL CHARACTERS.

BY

HENRY GREY.

EIGHTH THOUSAND.

THESE brief sketches of the Historical Novels by Sir Walter Scott,— whom Lord Meadowbank eulogised as ' The mighty magician who has rolled back the current of time, and conjured up before our living senses the men and manners of days which have long since passed away,'—are offered to the public with the hope that, to those who have read the Tales (which fill ten thousand closely - printed pages, and extend over a period of more than seven hundred years), they may serve as a memento of the principal scenes and characters ; and to those who have not, as an appetising foretaste of the intellectual feast in store for them.

OPINIONS OF THE PRESS.

' Surprisingly well done.'—*Banbury Guardian.*

' The entire essence of the stories.'—*Bedfordshire Mercury.*

' Each novel is condensed in a masterly manner.'—*Belfast News Letter.*

' Lovers of Scott will be greatly interested.'—*Boston Guardian.*

' Will tempt many to read the novels.'—*Boston Independent.*

' Admirably recalls the charming romances.'—*Bury and Norwich Post.*

' A very convenient refresher.'—*Cape Argus.*

' A useful little brochure.'—*Carlisle Express.*

' Gives a very good idea of the novels.'—*Chatham News.*

' Enough for obtaining an outline of the stories.'—*City Press.*

' A valuable and exceedingly handy little work.'—*Court Journal.*

OPINIONS OF THE PRESS, contd.

'A very useful little publication.'—*Dorset County Chronicle.*

'Reflects much credit on its author.'—*Dumfries Standard.*

'A novel idea well carried out.'—*Durham Chronicle.*

'We heartily commend this very happy idea.'—*Ecclesiastical Gazette.*

'Another useful work by Mr. Grey.'—*Edinburgh Courant.*

'Most pleasantly and accurately summarised.'—*Falkirk Herald.*

'An admirable idea carried out with great literary skill.'—*Farmer.*

'Will no doubt prove useful to readers of Scott.'—*Glasgow Herald.*

'The leading points are well brought out.'—*Grantham Journal.*

'The plot of each novel is carefully condensed in as few words as possible.'—*Graphic.*

'Concise, but thoroughly understandable.'—*Gravesend and Dartford Reporter.*

'Compiled with great tact and taste.'—*Greenock Herald.*

'Very skilfully and attractively epitomised.'—*Hampshire Telegraph.*

'Condensed with great skill.—*Hants and Berks Gazette.*

'A marvel of compactness.'—*Harper's Magazine.*

'A good idea well carried out.'—*Hertfordshire Mercury.*

'Written in a very attractive manner.'—*Jersey Express.*

'A curious and entertaining pamphlet.'—*Judy.*

'An exceedingly well-written summary.'—*Kentish Independent.*

'Will lead persons to read the novels instead of the trash in circulating libraries.'—*Life.*

'Gives a clear idea of each plot without spoiling the story.'—*Louth Times.*

'Admirably compiled.'—*Manchester Courier.*

'A clever sketch.'—*Modern Society.*

'Enough to recall the stories to those who have read them.'—*Montrose Standard.*

'Gives a clear outline of the tales.'—*Newport Advertiser.*

'The plots are clearly set forth.'—*New York Critic.*

'Will often be found of great assistance.'—*Northern Ensign.*

'Another proof of Mr. Grey's talent for epitomising.'—*North Sussex Gazette.*

'The principal scenes are vividly sketched.'—*North Wales Guardian.*

'A handy reminder of the mighty magician's creations.'—*Nottingham Guardian.*

'Will be welcomed by a large class of readers.'— *Ontario Chronicle.*

'Written in a very pleasing style.'—*Orcadian.*

'Will be read with interest and advantage.'—*Oxford Chronicle.*

'Gives a lucid outline of the plots.'—*Oxford and Cambridge Undergraduates' Journal.*

'Very successfully condensed.'—*People's Journal, Dundee.*

'A very careful summary.'—*St. Andrew's Gazette.*

'Very creditably accomplished.'—*Schoolmaster.*

'Gives a very pithy outline of each tale.'—*School Newspaper.*

'Most useful and accurate.'—*Shrewsbury Chronicle.*

'A most welcome and eminently successful work.'—*Shropshire Guardian.*

'A valuable appendage to the novels.'—*Sligo Chronicle.*

'A very useful compilation.'—*Society.*

'Will interest and be useful to everybody.'—*South London Press.*

'Well condensed and arranged.'—*Suburban Press.*

'Fits into the wards of each story in the smoothest fashion.'—*Sunday Times.*

'A handy little brochure.'—*Sussex Advertiser.*

'Well summarised.'—*Sussex Daily News.*

'Capitally done.'—*Tablet.*

'Unlocks several historical obscurities.'—*Wakefield Herald.*

'A perfect example of the art of condensation.'—*Warminster Herald.*

'May be thoroughly relied upon for its accuracy.'—*Warrington Examiner.*

'An excellent summary.'—*Warwick Advertiser.*

'The plot of each story may be learnt almost at a glance.'—*Wellington Weekly News.*

'Will be welcome to all who have an affection for the novels.'—*West of England Observer.*

'Admirably compiled.'—*Western Times.*

'Of real value for easy reference.'—*Westmorland Gazette.*

'Pithily and carefully written.'—*Winchester Observer.*

'A veritable *multum in parvo.*'—*Worcestershire Chronicle.*

'Will be valued by a large class of readers.'—*Yorkshire Chronicle.*

www.ingramcontent.com/pod-product-compliance
Lightning Source LLC
Chambersburg PA
CBHW032200010726
47493CB00008BA/2765